ABALONE
FROM SEA TO SAUCEPAN

PETE HUISVELD, KURT SCHMITT & MITZI & RED HOWARD

ILLUSTRATIONS BY DASHWOOD

TOFUA PRESS

COMMON ABALONE SHELLS
OF SOUTHERN CALIFORNIA

from the collection of

Hugh and Marge Bradner

WHITE *Haliotis sorenseni*

PINK *Haliotis corrugata*

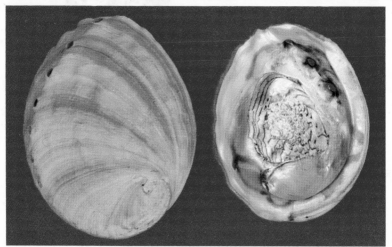

RED *Haliotis rufescens*

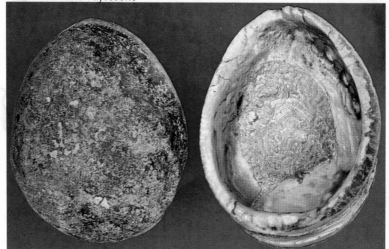

GREEN *Haliotis fulgens*

BLACK *Haliotis cracherodii*

Our basic abalone preparation uses flour, egg, and cracker crumbs. A smooth-faced pounder we cut out of a baseball bat tenderizes the steak by stretching and flattening it.

A good Chenin Blanc complements a dinner of "Standard Steaks."

photos by Eric Masterman

Abalone from Sea to Saucepan

Published by Tofua Press
10457-F Roselle Street
San Diego, California 92121

Printed in the United States of America.
All rights reserved.
Second edition, 1978.

Library of Congress Catalog Card Number 77-94788
ISBN: Cloth, 0-914488-19-8; paper, 0-914488-16-3

Editors: Diane Polster and Elizabeth Rand

Originally published by The Diving Dirtball Co., San Diego,
California

CONTENTS

Introduction   9
Once Upon a Time . . .   11
Hide 'n' Seek   16
   Excerpts from the 1978 California Fish and Game
     Regulations   18
   Guide to Common Southern California Abalone   19
The Naked Ab   25
Blood 'n' Guts   30
The Galloping Gastropod   36
   Standard Steaks à la S.I.O.   38
   Abalone Rellenos   40
   Pineapple roll   41
   Red's Steaks   42
   Abalone Aspic Salad   44
   Abalone Mexicana   45
   Abalone Saltimbocca   46
   Abalone Cordon Bleu   48
   Ab-burgers   50
   Teriyaki Ab   51
   Abalone Dirtballs   52
   Abalone Won Ton   54
   Ab Chowder   56
   Easy Soups   58
   Butter-fried Ab   59
   Abalone Sunrise   60

Bar-B-Q Ab   62
Abalone Creole   63
Sweet and Sour Abalone   64
Baked Ab   65
Perlemoen   66
Abalone Marsala   68
Abalone Thermidor   70
Abalone Newberg   71
AB-dendum   72
AB-ilogue   74
AB-pendix   77
Bibliography   79

INTRODUCTION

This book is written for just about everyone—beginner or pro. We thought about the soggy diver who spent two tanks of air prying up rocks and who, when he finally did find a real abalone, or "ab," discovered that it shared its home with a most unfriendly moray eel. We hope that it will be some small help to that up-and-coming new heroine, the ab-widow. Not totally unlike the familiar golf or football widow, this understanding lady puts up with lonely weekends, bathtubs full of wetsuits, muddy kitchen floors, and spattered drainboards, not to mention disaster-area kitchens besmithered by gallons of dirty Wesson Oil. And finally, we wrote this book for those fortunate friends and neighbors of divers who, without expending any energy of their own, are blessed with fresh, free abalone from overzealous divers who did manage to "limit out."

Abalone is a unique delicacy tasting like nothing else that comes from the sea. And the best abalone are found just off the coast of California. Gourmets know it as California's Golden Gastropod, or as the Sirloin of the Sea. To us, abalone was our staple food during our lean years of student life; it was our manna from the ocean.

The Diving Dirtballs are a curious lot. There is Pete, our chef and diving ace. (To qualify as an "ace," you must pop your limit of four legal abalone on one breath-hold dive.) Kurt "Bob Hope" Schmitt is our southpaw pounder. Then there's Red, our diving instructor, who can't even mix beer and egg without completely destroying the kitchen. Mitzi, our ab-widow, felt so sorry for Red that she finally married him. We are deeply indebted to Dr. Dave Leighton, an honest-to-Betsy authority on abalone, who pointed out so many errors in our original manuscript that we did not dare let him see the final version. And we acknowledge the spiritual support of the Adolph Coors Company, which made long evenings at the typewriter so much longer.

The recipes listed are varied to suit your enthusiasm, skill, and time. They're not really hard once you get the hang of it. As Mitzi says, "If you can read, you can cook—probably."

ONCE UPON A TIME...

Scientists claim that abalone have been around for over 100 million years. Now when you consider that an abalone grows about an inch each year, the ab that's been around for that long could cover the ocean floor from here to Japan! This, of course, accounts for any mother-of-pearl that might be drilled up by the Deep Sea Drilling Project. Mitzi claims that it might even provide the driving mechanism for continental drift.

Abalone can be found off the eastern coasts of Russia, but despite any claims, they were not first invented there. Back when the Greeks were perfecting the arts of argument and politics, Aristotle wrote of a "wild limpet" which many then called the "sea ear." Even today, the English know abalone by the name "Venus's Ear." The artist Brueghel included an abalone shell in one of his paintings in 1604. And while the Western world was talking about and painting abalone, the Japanese were already making money at it with a commercial fishery that dates back to 425 A.D.

Our favorite aspect of the Japanese fishery is that the actual diving is still done only by the fishermen's wives. This is perhaps due to the ancient Japanese belief that diving causes sterility in men. The belief is, of course, more prevalent among the lazier men, but we suspect that maybe the old Oriental doctor who first had this idea was not all that dumb. We heard it rumored that this same doctor also suggested that acupuncture be used to treat the dreaded divers' disease, "the bends." The theory was that the needles could pop the bubbles that had formed in the diver's tissue.

"Ama" means "women sea divers" in Japan, where for more than a thousand years these taut-skinned young women have been diving naked in the blue sea and bathing in the sunlight after their hard work. The Ama's ancient communities are now quickly disappearing from Japan. But the picture of Oriental girls skinny-dipping for abalone is so stirring that Kurt, traditionalist that he is, is already planning to preserve this honorable life style in his backyard swimming pool. Remember James Bond in *You Only Live Twice?* Kurt says, "you only live once!"

The Japanese call their abalone "awabi" and they are, naturally, shorter than the abalone off the coast of western North America. Nevertheless, the Japanese have named one of their species *Haliotis gigantea.*

The greatest number of different species is found in the south and central Pacific. In Australia, abalone is called "mutton fish," and in New Zealand it's "paua." Even though abalone are found around most of the Pacific islands, they simply refuse to live in Hawaii. All attempts to establish abalone there by transplanting young ones from California have failed. They probably can't afford the rent.

Some of the larger species are found off the coasts of South Africa, where abalone is called "perlemoen." Abalone range into the Atlantic to the Canary Islands and the Azores. Only one species is native to the shores of the Mediterranean Sea, and only a single species ranges northward along France and among the British Isles.

Abalone are not found in the Gulf of California or the Gulf of Mexico, nor along South America, Central America, or the eastern seaboard of North America. Well, there have been some exceptions. Abalone are found on the Galapagos Islands, which are always an exception to anything. An empty shell

World Distribution of Abalone

*Abalones are found among islands
and along coastlines of continents
within solid black lines*

was picked up on the beach of Copacabana, Rio de Janiero, Brazil. Scientists promptly named it, catalogued it, and still argue over its classification. We suggest the name *Haliotis lostus*. Two small individuals were dredged up in deep water near Key West, Florida—one in 1869 and the other in 1913. No doubt these were a couple of vacationing abs from Europe on their way to the Copacabana beach.

There is a mollusk the Chileans call the "Chilean abalone," or "loco." But it's not really an abalone. It looks like one, tastes almost like one, doesn't smell like one, and even eats crabs. It's really a seagoing carniverous snail. But Dr. Dave is planning to introduce California abalone into Chilean waters, so Chile may some day have real abalone.

Abalone were fished for many years by the Indians along the southwest coast of North America and the Channel Islands. The Portuguese explorer Juan Rodriguez Cabrillo raved about a shellfish dinner provided by local Indians shortly after he discovered San Diego Harbor in 1542. Indians in the central and northwest central regions of California used the shells in their jewelry and knives. They called the shells "uhello," the same name they used for the money they fabricated from them. We are still trying to reestablish this old Indian tradition, but today the abalone meat is worth a lot more uhello than the shells.

When Chinese laborers were brought to California in the mid-nineteenth century to help build the railroads and work mines, they were the first non-Indians to appreciate the treasure that lay just off our shores. Back in China, the peasants were prohibited from fishing this delicacy. So here they excitedly worked from small skiffs in the intertidal areas knocking off the abalone with long poles. The Chinese initiated a new industry in America of drying the meat and exporting it to the Orient.

Americans as yet had so little desire for the delicate flavor that during the 1870s the shells were actually selling here at twice the price of the meat. Nonetheless, Americans were interested, since by 1900 California ordinances were passed making it unlawful to fish for abalone except in deeper water. Since the Chinese were not divers, in came the Japanese. First free-diving with only their traditional "sake barrel" floats, the Japanese soon brought over their hard-hat diving gear. It was not until the 1930s that any Caucasian divers were to master such abalone diving techniques. But considering the decompression schedules many of these honky divers are following, there is still some question as to whether they have ever mastered anything. Nevertheless, these divers continue to bring up abs from the deep water off the California coast.

Some 30 years ago, a California Indian named Dutch Pierce got his five brothers together to compete with the near monopoly of the Japanese-American divers. Today the Pierce processing and freezing plant in Santa Barbara is probably the most successful operation of its kind in the world. Yankee ingenuity now supplies abalone to the world's supermarkets, best hotels, and finest restaurants.

Today's sport fisherman can now use SCUBA south of Yankee Point in Monterey County, but you must "free dive" without this gear if you fish north of this point. Well, after all, the abalone are shallower up there and it wouldn't be sporting.

In 1945 it became illegal to export abalone meat from California. So if you didn't know any California divers then, you knew that the Mexicans called abalone "aulone." Even today the abalone caught off the coast of Baja California is one of Mexico's major seafood exports.

Some years after 1945 we gave some competition to Mexico by allowing the exportation of ground abalone trimmings. Then in 1968 the world was allowed to import a taste of California's shellfish steak.

A seagoing abalone looks much like your ordinary household rock, but it's covered with moss and barnacles and other marine growths, and has little tentacles sticking out around its flat foot. Some, or maybe it's only Red, have suggested that abalone are actually large, mutant killer snails produced by a mad scientist on some island in the Pacific.

There are over 130 species and subspecies of abalone in the world. The most common species found off Southern California are popularly called reds, greens, and pinks. There are some whites deeper and blacks shallower and a lot of crossbreeds. Whites are the most tender, so restaurants will always claim to be serving only whites. The pinks are next. The other species require more pounding than the whites or pinks to tenderize them. Some, often the greens, have a darker meat, but they all taste equally great. Blacks sometimes tend to be a bit tough, with about the texture of truck tire rubber.

California state regulations require that the abalone be taken only from a half hour before sunrise to a half hour after sunset. The sport divers' fishing season lasts from March 16 to January 14, which gives the diver ample opportunity to eat to his stomach's delight. We do not really know why the season is closed during the winter months. Most species of abalone usually spawn in the late summer and fall. Perhaps the

Department of Fish and Game does not want us to disturb the abs' rest.

The minimum length of a legal abalone for sport divers is now 7 inches for reds, 6 inches for greens, pinks, and whites, 5 inches for blacks, and 4 inches for all other species. The size is determined by the maximum shell diameter. These limits and other fishing regulations are continually changing, so when you purchase your annual fishing license be sure to pick up a copy of the current regulations. We have reproduced the 1978 regulations pertaining to abalone fishing on page 18.

Illegally small abalone are commonly called "shorts." Of course, the term "short" also applies to illegally young women who we're told also are protected by the Fish and Game Department—much to Kurt's dismay. Should you mistakenly pop off a short abalone, it must be put back. To do this you usually need to hold the ab against a rock until it regains its footing, which might take as long as a minute.

There are a number of methods for recognizing each species so as not to take an illegally small ab and get slapped with a five-million-dollar fine. Remember that juvenile abalone are flatter, and more colorful, like kids everywhere. Of course, you can always make sure each ab is at least 7 inches long, but this can become very discouraging if every one you find is 6 ⅞ inches. The shape of the shell, the inner shell trim color, the number of breathing holes, and the color of the foot and tentacles are all good things to look for—at least these can tell you whether or not you have a rock. Be on the lookout for the not-too-rare hybrids, which is what we call anything we can't identify.

Finding abalone is always the diver's first step to a great meal; that is, unless you get bounced in by the surf like Pete usually does—one small step for man, one giant leap for Pete. Discovering the right area is usually the biggest problem unless you are somewhere like San Clemente Island, where abalone are reported to live so abundantly that they com-

1978 California
Sport Fishing Regulations

LICENSE PROVISIONS

A fishing license is required of any person 16 years of age, or over; including members of the armed forces of the United States, for the taking of any kind of fish, mollusk, invertebrate, amphibian or crustacean in California, except of persons fishing from a public pier in waters of the Pacific Ocean (the public pier must be in the open sea adjacent to the coast and islands of California or in the waters of those open bays or enclosed bays contiguous to the ocean). No license is required for the taking of reptiles.

Invertebrates

29.05 **GENERAL:** (a) Except as provided in this article there are no closed seasons, bag limits, or minimum size limits for any invertebrate whose take is authorized in this article, and they may be taken at any time of day or night. In San Francisco and San Pablo bays and saltwater tributaries east of the Golden Gate Bridge invertebrates may not be taken at night except from the shore.

(b) Tidal invertebrates may not be taken in any tidepool or other areas between the high tide mark and 1,000 feet beyond the low tide mark without a written permit from the Department, except as follows:

(1) In state parks, state beaches, state recreation areas, state underwater parks, state reserves, national parks, national monuments or national seashores: Abalones, chiones, clams, cockles, crabs, lobsters, scallops, ghost shrimp and sea urchins may be taken. Worms may be taken except that no worms may be taken in any mussel bed, nor may any person disturb or damage mussels while taking worms.

(2) In all other areas, except where prohibited within marine life refuges or other special closures: Abalones, chiones, clams, cockles, crabs, limpets, lobsters, moon snails, mussels, sand dollars, octopi, shrimp, scallops, sea urchins, turban snails, squid and worms may be taken.

(3) Special Closure. No invertebrates shall be taken on the mainland shore within the boundaries of Año Nuevo State Reserve between the high tide mark and 100 feet beyond the low tide mark between November 30 and March 16.

(c) **Measuring Devices:** Every person while taking invertebrates which have a size limit shall carry a device which is capable of accurately measuring the size of the species taken.

(d) In all ocean waters skin and SCUBA divers may take invertebrates as provided in this article except that in all ocean waters north of Yankee Point (Monterey Co.), self-contained underwater breathing apparatus (SCUBA) may be used only to take sea urchins and rock scallops. For the purpose of this section, breathing tubes are not underwater artificial breathing devices.

MOLLUSKS

29.10 **GENERAL:** (a) Except as otherwise provided in this article, saltwater mollusks including octopus may be taken only on hook and line or with the hands.

(b) The size of a mollusk is measured in greatest shell diameter.

29.15 **ABALONE:** (a) **Limit:** Four in the combination of all species. Minimum size measured in greatest shell diameter: Red abalone seven inches; green abalone, pink abalone and white abalone six inches; black abalone five inches and all other species four inches. All legal size abalones detached must be retained and a person shall stop detaching abalones when bag limit is reached.

(b) **Open Season:** North of Yankee Point (Monterey Co.) abalone may be taken only during the months of April, May, June, August, September, October and November. South of Yankee Point abalone may be taken from March 16 through January 14 except as follows: (1) On the northeasterly side of Santa Catalina Island between the extreme westerly end and the United States Government Light on the southeasterly end, abalones may be taken only from April 1 to October 1. (2) Between Palos Verdes Point (Los Angeles Co.) and Dana Point (Orange Co.) abalone may not be taken at any time of the year.

(c) **Fishing hours:** One-half hour before sunrise to one-half hour after sunset only.

(d) **Abalones Retained:** No undersized abalone may be brought ashore or aboard any boat, placed in any type receiver, kept on the person, or retained in any person's possession or under his control. Undersize abalone must be replaced immediately with the shell outward to the surface of the rock from which detached. Abalones brought ashore shall be in such a condition that the size can be determined. Abalones not attached in the shell may not be transported or possessed, except when being prepared for immediate consumption.

(e) **Special gear provisions:** Abalone may be taken only by hand or by devices commonly known as abalone irons. Abalone irons must be less than 36 inches long, straight or with a curve having a radius of not less than 18 inches such as irons made from automobile leaf springs or similarly curved material, and must not be less than 3/4-inch wide nor less than 1/16-inch thick. All edges must be rounded and free of sharp edges. Knives, screwdrivers and sharp instruments are prohibited.

SPECIES	NO. & CHARACTER OF OPEN HOLES	SHELL	BODY	TYPICAL DEPTH IN FEET	COMMENTS
WHITE *H. sorenseni*	3 - 5 oval; highly elevated.	thin, circular; highly arched; purple edge; pearly white interior, no muscle scar.	long, thin, yellow-green tentacles; bright yellow-orange foot.	80 - 100	typically 5 - 8 inches in length; the premium; tender meat requires little or no pounding; not found north of Pt. Conception.
PINK *H. corrugata*	2 - 4 round; highly elevated.	circular; corrugated, scalloped edge & shell; thick layer of red-brown with green or blue zones; large muscle scar with pink reflections.	long, slender jet-black tentacles with distinct white area between tentacles; cream-colored foot; mottled tan and black epipodium.	20 - 80	usually everything but pink; known in Mexico as "yellow" abalone; average size 6 inches.
RED *H. rufescens*	3 - 5 oval; elevated.	lumpy, undulating; thick red layer with red rim.	black tentacles with black area between; brown foot.	50 - 80	found shallower (0 - 10 feet) further north; largest of all ab species, may approach a foot in length; most sought-after species.
GREEN *H. fulgens*	5 - 7 round; barely raised	oval; olive green to red-brown; shows considerable variation; pearly white inside with blue and green reflections.	short, thick beige-green tentacles with dark areas between; brown foot.	10 - 20	generally considered to have the most beautiful shell interior; known in Mexico as "blue" abalone; typically 5 - 8 inches in length.
BLACK *H. cracherodii*	5 - 9 round; flush	black; smooth with little marine growth, pearly white interior; no muscle scar.	black epipodium with grayish-green or greenish-gray foot.	0 - 10	hardiest species, endures intertidal surf and repeated air exposure at low tides; average size 3 - 5 inches.

Note: No single characteristic is completely reliable in providing unique identification. Species' individuals may also vary considerably from one or more features listed.

pletely cover the rocks on which they live. Such is not the case along the California coast, where you still have to work for your dinner.

Abs are usually found hanging around under rock ledges or other protected areas within rock formations. Their local distribution is very patchy. You could spend an entire day in one likely area of rocks searching in vain, while only a few yards away under the next ledge the abs are holding a convention. There are some great places for abs to live that we have come across, but apparently the abs don't know about them.

And finding an ab does not assure the diver of his prize. The ab may be so far under the ledge that it is impossible to reach him, or that big moray eel lurking next to his prey may prove discouraging—in fact, downright painful!

For these reasons skin divers need to know precisely where to find their prey, and they hope it will be in shallow water, otherwise they could easily become exhausted in a futile search for dinner. SCUBA, of course, allows a much greater range of exploration, vertically as well as horizontally, as long as you don't go horizontally north of Yankee Point.

The sport diver can always be found carrying his fishing license and ab iron, a straight or slightly curved iron at least ¾-inch wide, ¹/₁₆-inch thick, and about a foot long. It's usually made of aluminum, but we still call it an iron. It is with this clever device of engineering brilliance that most divers remove abalone from rocks. For you lazier types, Red fully understands your needs, and is working on a pneumatic ab-iron that is powered from his scuba tank and blows the abs off the rocks.

Being a gastropod, and moving around rocks on its foot, the abalone is capable of employing strong suction to virtually clamp its shell to a rock. The diver may then find it almost impossible to get his iron between the shell and the rock. You can try tickling its tentacles with a leaf of kelp, its favorite food. The idea is to get the abalone rolling on its back, screaming for you to stop. Theory has it that a 6-inch abalone

can suck with a force equal to 400 pounds! But once a small amount of the iron is under the shell, there is a great deal of leverage at the diver's command and the ab may then be pried off the rock. Of course, if the diver is quick enough, the ab can be popped before it can react and clamp down on the rock. And there are a few divers who with great speed and coordination pluck the critters from the rocks with their bare hands. Modesty should prohibit us from naming any, but once while Pete was free-diving, he was just able to get his fingers under a shell when it suddenly clamped down. There he was, stuck and out of breath, with nothing to do but wait for a low tide.

One marine biologist spent an enormous sum of somebody's money to determine that abalone do not move more than a few feet in any direction during their lifetimes. We could have told them that for a quarter. The end result is that you should remember where you leave your "shorts."

More often than not, the diver finds himself upside down peering under a ledge through the dirty water and a half-flooded mask, struggling against the bottom surge to maintain his position, breathing out of a near empty tank, tangled in kelp and suffering incredible pain. He is conscious only of his quarry, oblivious to all these other problems. Any diver will readily tell you about that huge ab just out of reach under some rock ledge that he almost had when he ran out of air. If only he had had a slightly longer iron. . . .

The fact is, somewhere out there, the "Monster Ab" waits patiently to pounce on his next unsuspecting diver. If it had only a slightly longer pounce, we might never have returned from that last dive. In the 1 April 1965 issue of *Skin Diver Magazine* a report of a mammoth catch was supported by a photograph showing a 48-inch ab weighing 149 pounds, 8½ ounces. The report read ". . .the reef began to move."

Abalone that a diver does catch are carefully placed in the diver's "goodie bag," which now becomes the diver's most valued possession. Divers have been seen rolling in heavy surf

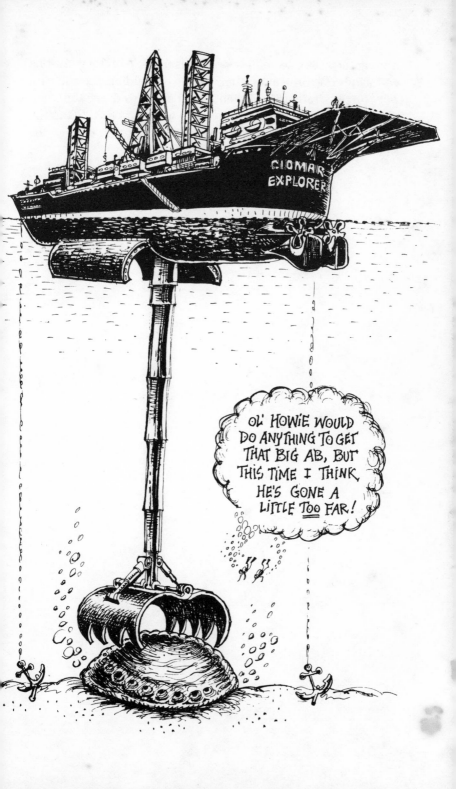

among the rocks, seemingly oblivious to the pain they must be enduring, not protecting their heads or holding their masks, but clinging stalwartly to their bag of abs. The divers' buddies, already ashore, see their friends in trouble and rush out to the rescue. Note that it is always the goodie bag that they go for first.

THE NAKED AB

The abalone is a gastropod mollusk that belongs to the genus *Haliotis*. Are you ready? Abalones belong to the class Gastropoda, subclass Prosobranchia, order Archaegastropoda, suborder Zygobranchia, superfamily Pleurotomariacae, and family Haliotidae. But don't bother about all this; it gives jobs to biologists and is thus good for the economy. For our purposes, we shall tell you a little about the abs' anatomy and physiology as it is applicable to their consumption (ahh. . .).

Abs are pretty simple creatures. Their nervous system is relatively primitive, so you don't really need to worry about hurting the little beasties. All around their foot they have short tentacles which are sensitive to touch and probably to chemicals, especially the scent of kelp. They also have small eyes on short eye stalks, and organs of balance called statocysts, which may not work too well, since abs are often found hanging upside down. As with all mollusks, their circulatory system is open, that is, all the vessels dump into a reservoir-like area which then drains back towards the heart. The blood is clear to milkish with a slight tinge of blue. There is no mechanism to coagulate the blood, so if it is deeply cut, the ab may bleed to death. For this reason, you are not allowed to use your dive-knife to pry abalone from their rocks.

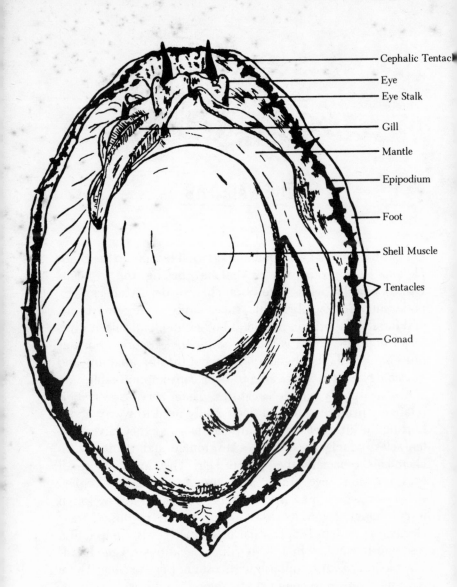

Cephalic Tentacle

Eye

Eye Stalk

Gill

Mantle

Epipodium

Foot

Shell Muscle

Tentacles

Gonad

Dorsal view of abalone with shell removed.

From California Department of Fish and Game
Fish Bulletin no. 118 by Keith W. Cox.

26

Abalone blood contains antimicrobial properties that are effective against a wide variety of microorganisms including penicillin-resistant *Staphylococcus aureus* and certain polio and influenza viruses. So wethinks that perhaps an abalone diet can provide some immunity from the flu epidemics that periodically hit Southern California.

The part of the ab that we're most interested in is the muscle. The biggest portion is the foot, its fringing "epipodium," and the right columellar muscle, which attaches the foot to the shell. This is what you eat—it's pure meat with no gristle, fat, or waste.

As far as the critter's internal and digestive anatomy goes, we're not going to go into the gruesome detail that we're known for at the dinner table. Although you might not have noticed, abs have little heads with little mouths and a file-like structure called radula that serves as teeth. They need this since they graze on kelp, of all things.

No story would be complete without a few words about the romance and sex life of the abalone. After all, baby abs have to come from somewhere and the stork is not a likely prospect (would you believe the dolphin?). First of all, there are boy-abs and girl-abs to make things fun. Each has a large horn-shaped gonad; the male's is creamy beige and the female's is greenish. Abs apparently don't breed until they are about 3.5 inches long (or about 9 centimeters, 0.05 fathoms, or 0.0004 furlongs). The males, as usual, start first. Pinks and greens spawn most vigorously from summer through early fall, and some species can spawn all year round, depending on their geographical location and the water temperature. Anyway, they mate in the traditional aquatic manner, by spraying their sperm and ova in a "shotgun" manner.

Baby abs are very small, swim for about a week, then settle down to a lazy bottom life. As they grow, they get more holes, which are arranged in a spiral—you can see the old, filled-in ones on a clean shell. The open holes allow sea water to pass over the gills and, when viewed from the outside, always spiral outward in a clockwise direction. It is amazing that viewed from the inside these same holes spiral outward in a counterclockwise direction! Legal-sized abs are usually 7 to 8 years old, but the growth rate varies a great deal, depending on the food available and the water temperature. Diet also affects the color of the shells, and varying bands of color on an ab shell are probably the result of changes in diet.

Let us say that it seems that abalone were created just for us. They are relatively easy to catch—not find, but catch. They are almost pure meat, have functional and lovely shells, and taste fantastic.

Now if we could train them to come when we called. . . .

BLOOD 'N' GUTS!

Returning from a successful dive, the ab-er's next step toward dinner is the cleaning of the abalone. This does not involve Ajax or steel wool, though Red tried this once.

To clean an abalone the animal must be removed from its shell. Once Pete tried to pound an ab while it was still in the shell. He ended up breading the abalone in shell crumbs.

The ab is connected to its shell at the top of its muscle in a roughly circular area about 3 inches in diameter. To remove the ab from its shell, place a wooden spoon between the abalone and the shell and shove it along the shell's inner surface. Don't use a metal spoon since it will cut the abalone and probably bend the spoon.

It is quite possible to pop abs out of their shells by hand. If you want to try this, allow the abalone to relax first. This is done by propping the ab up on its end. The ab will then start to "come out and look around." Or you can hold the ab by the shell with the foot down and wait for it to relax. While it's doing this, sneakily and gently grasp the shell and forcefully slide your thumb or fingers between the abalone and the shell. Great care should be taken while doing this, since the edges are sharp. If you're careless, remember that abalone do not have red blood, so if you see any, it's yours. If abs are relaxed, they come out of the shell fairly easily. If they know you're coming you might have to fight all day. Take Red's word for it.

We hear that if an abalone is left in a cool place for an entire day it will be very easy to remove from the shell and easier to pound. We have never let any abs sit around that long, since Pete would have starved while we waited. However, the commercial ab people do it, as well as many other sport divers, so you might want to give it a try.

Next take the organism and excise the viscera—i.e., cut off the guts. Now trim off the dark portions around the foot, and "skin" the abalone. The diagram below should help to explain how the abalone should be skinned. The solid line is before, and the dotted line is after trimming. Some divers prefer to finish trimming the sides after slicing the abalone into steaks. Kurt, "the knife," says when you trim, you should trim. He likes leaving all his fingers in one place.

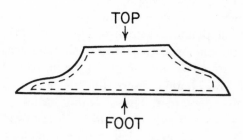

In the cross section shown, notice that the sole of the foot must also be removed, because it is extremely tough. There has been some discussion of using it for shoe leather, but the smell of old dried-out abalone is worse than Pete's socks. For all this trimming a very, very sharp knife is a real advantage, if not a necessity.

Now there are two important points: (1) the trimmings and slop get ripe pretty fast, permanently odorizing the house; (2) modern technology has yet to produce a garbage disposal that is a match for the foot and other epipodial debris. Therefore, we promptly dump everything into a plastic bag and hermetically seal it in a garbage can.

31

The recipes usually require what are called "steaks." These are cut by slicing the abalone horizontally, parallel to its foot, into about ¼-inch slices. If something other than steaks is called for, first cut the steaks, pound them, and then grind, dice, or whatever. A meat slicer is neat. Or you can use a cutting board onto which you've nailed two small pieces of wood, ¼-inch thick, and joined in a "V." To use this, simply slide the abalone into the V and run your sharp knife along the top of the nailed-on piece.

If you're brave, or have uncuttable fingers, you can try to cut the steaks using just your knife. Kurt was only brave. Depending on the size of the ab, and the thickness of the steaks you cut, the yield should be 4 to 7 steaks from each ab.

Now comes the pounding, best done at a reasonable, neighborly hour. With the exception of the very tender whites, the meat is tough and needs to be tenderized. Even the tough meat, however, is very delicate and tears easily. So use the flat side of a meat pounder, and a drawing or pulling motion; otherwise you end up with pounded abalone grits. We have found that a 3-inch section cut out of the fat part of a baseball bat, with a dowel handle inserted in the side, makes an ideal and inexpensive pounder. The Al Kaline, Mickey Mantle, or Hank Aaron special models seem to tenderize especially well. (If you don't have a baseball bat, a rubber mallet also works.)

While pounding the steaks, you will find that they enjoy jumping out from under the pounder. Their current record is across the kitchen, over the river and through the woods. . . .

The steaks must be pounded until limp. For breaded steaks a little extra pounding is desirable. The steak will spread out as it is pounded. Again, it will help if a slight pulling or drawing motion is used while pounding, to help tenderize and prevent splitting the steak. There are a few old salts who insist on a paper-thin steak that covers the entire kitchen counter. This is not really necessary.

Abalone can be frozen whole, after slicing, or even after it has been pounded. Wrap it in plastic and then in freezer wrap and put it in the freezer. Wait for one of those days when the

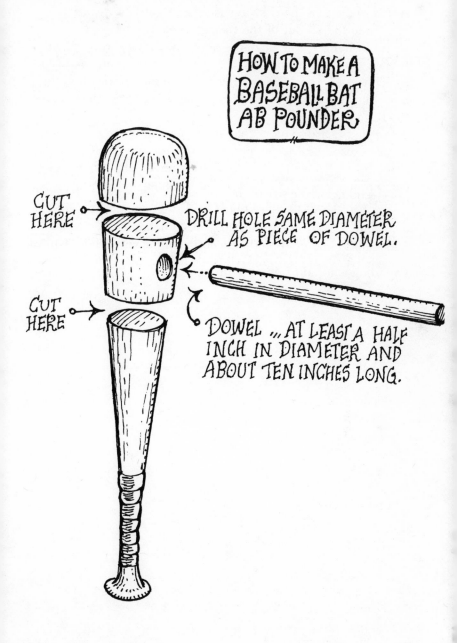

HOW TO MAKE A
BASEBALL BAT
AB POUNDER.

CUT HERE

DRILL HOLE SAME DIAMETER AS PIECE OF DOWEL.

CUT HERE

DOWEL ... AT LEAST A HALF INCH IN DIAMETER AND ABOUT TEN INCHES LONG.

surf is so big that the US Navy isn't letting its aircraft carriers out. Take the ab out of the freezer, soak your wetsuit in the bathtub, hang it out in plain sight, and invite some diving friends over for an abalone dinner. Abalone that has been frozen fresh is nearly as good as fresh. In fact, some think the later thawing enhances the tenderness, though it slightly dulls the flavor.

We had heard rumors that if an abalone were connected across a car battery, pounding would no longer be needed. Pete broke out his jumper cables, then broke a tooth trying to eat our test-case ab. Old wooden washing machine rollers have shown great potential for quickly tenderizing steaks, and as quickly flattening fingers. Not even the commercial fisheries have figured out a way to automate this pounding, so if you discovered any new techniques, please let us know. Pounding is a pain in the thumb.

THE GALLOPING GASTROPOD

We call the following basic abalone cooking rules "The Big Four":

1. ALWAYS pound your abalone.

Once you have sliced the abalone into steaks, pound them immediately, before freezing or before you start any of the recipes. (For an exception to this rule, see recipe on page 66.) Remember always to use a pulling motion so as not to split or crack the meat.

2. NEVER overcook. If in doubt, undercook.

Failure to follow the above two rules will cause what we in the business call a "wallet." This is a highly complicated concept which can best be explained by a little experiment. Place your hand on the thing you carry your money in. Now take a large bite and chew thoroughly. We'll wait. Now, what did that taste like? It doesn't matter, because it's just plain tough. It would be a shame for your abalone to end up like that.

3. ALWAYS degrease your oil-fried abalone.

Drain it on paper bags or by patting with paper towels.

4. NEVER count on our numbers.

We have tried to give you some basic idea of how many servings there are in each recipe. Now we all know that this is just not possible. First, a standard recipe that "serves 6" won't feed two of us. Second, what we can eat varies significantly from one day to the next. Take our estimations only as a guide.

By the way, California vintners recommend Chenin Blanc to accompany an abalone dish. It is indeed an excellent accompaniment.

We recommend Coors.

And always remind yourself—if the Diving Dirtballs can cook it, you can cook it.

Standard Steaks à la S.I.O.
(The specialty of the Scripps Institution of Oceanography)

This is the basic, though not the easiest, way of cooking abalone. On a plate put a small amount of flour. In a bowl beat a couple of eggs and just a little beer. (The beer is what makes it the specialty of many Scripps divers.) In another, large bowl put some very finely crushed cracker crumbs. If you're rich, use Chicken-in-a-Biskit crackers. These have the best consistency and flavor. If you're broke, use the cheapest soda crackers you can find and season with a little garlic powder, onion powder, and celery salt. Do this to taste. If you don't notice the spices when you smell the cracker crumbs, add some more. If the smell of the spices is very strong, crunch up more crackers.

Dip the ab steaks into the flour, then the egg, and then the crumbs. Press the crumbs firmly onto the abalone to make sure they stick. This can be done an hour or so before your guests arrive so you have time to clean up the mess.

Fry the steaks in ½ inch of hot oil for about 20 seconds on the first side, 20 seconds on the second side, and 10 more seconds on the first side. The exact timing will vary with the temperature of the oil and the thickness of the steak, and you want the cracker crumbs to be brown and crisp. Drain on paper towels and serve immediately.

Many people like to serve this with a very mild cheese or Hollandaise sauce. Just be careful to accent and not smother the abalone's delicate flavor.

If you make more of these than you can eat, don't worry. Wrap and refrigerate the leftover steaks. They are great the next day, warmed or cold, plain or in a sandwich. Kurt prefers his with Heinz ketchup, but then he prefers everything with ketchup.

Five steaks per person is usually plenty, but that will depend upon the size of the steaks. We usually talk our guests into bringing a salad. Potato chips with an avocado dip can then complete the dinner.

One of our favorites.

"ER...THAT'S NOT EXACTLY WHAT I HAD IN MIND WHEN I TOLD YOU TO BRING ALONG A GOOD AB IRON!"

Abalone Rellenos

(say: ray-AY-nose)

Bread your largest steaks according to the recipe on page 38, but don't cook them yet. Near one edge of the steak, place a spoonful of Ortega diced chiles and spread in a straight line near that edge of the steak. On top of this place some grated Mozarella cheese, and then add just a little Ragu spaghetti sauce. Now roll the steak so all the gunk winds up in the middle of the rolled steak. If you can't figure this out (you should have seen Pete's first one), simply cut a piece of paper in a roughly circular shape. Now place a pencil on the piece of paper and roll the paper around the pencil. Now, class, the piece of paper is the abalone and the pencil is the glop. If you've gotten this far with the real thing, stick one or two toothpicks through the relleno to hold it together. Fry this in a covered frying pan with about ¼ inch of medium-hot oil. Roll the relleno frequently (for even cooking) until the cheese is melted, usually about 3 minutes.

These can be enhanced with a cheese sauce, and when served with a salad can make a most filling meal. We each usually eat 2 to 4 of these rellenos.

This is the recipe that prompted everyone to say: "You should write a book!" or "You should go into the restaurant business!" So we wrote a book. Putting Red in a kitchen would just be inviting disaster. Besides, we could never have kept the waitresses.

pineapple roll

Prepare and cook the same as Abalone Rellenos, but use drained crushed pineapple as the filling. Now we realize that this sounds kind of weird. Give it a try. It's really quite good, unless you hate pineapple.

Red's Steaks

This is a much easier way of cooking steaks, but not quite as good as the Standard Steaks à la SIO, page 38.

	pounded abalone steaks
1	cup milk
1	egg
1¼	cup white flour
½	teaspoon salt
1	teaspoon seasoned salt

Mix all of the above, except the abalone, together in a bowl. Then place some more flour on a plate. Dip steaks into the flour and then into the batter. Fry in hot oil until the batter is light brown.

Can be served as a entrée with any of your leftover side dishes. If it's been a really long day of surf-diving, this may be just the recipe.

Abalone Aspic Salad

¼ pound abalone, pounded and ground
2 envelopes unflavored gelatin
2 cups Clamato juice or substitute 1½
   cups V-8 and ½ cup clam juice
3 tablespoons lemon juice
   dash pepper

Bring ⅔ cup water to a boil and add the abalone. Remove from heat after one minute and drain, saving the liquid. Put gelatin in ½ cup cold water; stir until gelatin is moistened. Place over low heat and stir constantly until gelatin is dissolved, about 5 minutes.

Remove from heat and stir in the Clamato juice, lemon juice, abalone water, and pepper. Chill until mixture starts to thicken, and then stir in the abalone. Chill until firm.

Now let us explain that this is not all that easy. If you add the abalone too soon, it all winds up on the bottom of the salad. If you add it too late, you have a gelatin salad with some abalone sort of "plopped" on top. It becomes downright frustrating when it jells too much and you have to melt it in a warm place—again too much, rechill it—too much, warm—well, you get the idea. Just keep an eye on it and do it right the first time. Of course, it tastes just as good no matter where the abalone ends up!

Abalone Mexicana

This is the recipe that won Congressman Bob Wilson of the 40th Congressional District of San Diego, California, a "Chef of the West" award from *Sunset Magazine* in February 1961. It is printed with his permission.

1	pound abalone steaks, pounded
2	eggs, beaten
½	cup tomato sauce
¾	cup medium-coarse soda cracker crumbs
¼	cup green pepper, chopped fine
	paprika
	salt to taste

Marinate the abalone steaks in mixture of beaten eggs and tomato sauce for at least 30 minutes. Remove steaks from the marinade and cover each side with cracker crumbs. Sprinkle each breaded steak lightly with chopped green pepper, pressing the green pepper and cracker crumbs firmly into the abalone to make sure they stick. Sprinkle with paprika to taste.

Fry in a buttered, medium-hot skillet for not more than 1 minute on each side. Then salt to taste. Serve on a hot plate garnished with lemon or lime slices. Serves 4.

Abalone Saltimbocca
(That's Italian for "jump inna the mouth")

6	thin slices each of ham and Swiss cheese
12	abalone steaks, pounded
¼	cup grated Parmesan cheese
¼	cup flour
½	teaspoon powdered sage (this is supposed to make the Saltimbocca)
½	teaspoon salt
¼	teaspoon pepper
	some flour
2	eggs, beaten well with 2 tablespoons milk
2	tablespoons oil
2	tablespoons butter
1	10 ½-ounce can condensed cream of chicken soup
½-¾	cup white wine (we use cheap Sauterne, and so can afford to use a bit more of it—but only ½ cup of the good stuff)

Trim the slices of ham and cheese so that they're about ¼-inch smaller than the steaks. Then make ham and cheese sandwiches using two steaks for the bread (hold the mustard and mayo). [Red next wanted to make Monte Cristo style ab sandwiches. If you don't know what a Monte Cristo sandwich is, that's good, because Mitzi didn't like the idea and wanted to make something more like a Cordon Bleu. Kurt liked Red's idea and Pete always likes a fight. Mitzi won. Red now calls this "abalone cordon black-and-bleu."]

If you want to make this look fancier than stuffed steaks, or if you only have 6 steaks and can't divide by 2, lay a slice of ham and cheese on top of each steak and roll up with the ham and cheese on the inside. Secure the steak with toothpicks.

Mix the Parmesan cheese with the ¼ cup flour, sage, salt, and pepper. Dip the "sandwiches" or rolls in flour, then into the egg, and finally into the Parmesan cheese mix. Press the coating firmly onto the abalone to help it stick. You should refrigerate these at least 1 hour, and can even leave them there overnight.

Preheat oven to 300°F. Heat the oil and butter in a skillet. Lightly brown the sandwiches or rolls on all sides. Place them in a single layer in a shallow casserole dish. Pour on the sauce made by mixing the condensed soup with the wine. Then heat in the oven for 15 minutes, or you can put the rolls and sauce in a Crock Pot slow cooker for about 2 hours. We always use too much wine and need to thicken the sauce with a bit of the Parmesan cheese mixture.

Serves 3¼.

Abalone Cordon Bleu

Our thanks to the Sea Thief Restaurant in La Jolla for sharing this recipe. The Sea Thief chef told us that it was an unwitting patron who, upon tasting abalone for the first time, remarked that its texture and subtle flavor were reminiscent of veal. Since Abalone Parmigiana is prepared in some places, the chef thought, "What about an Abalone Cordon Bleu?"

For each serving:

1	thin slice of ham, prosciutto if you can get it
1	thin slice of Provolone or Swiss cheese
2	abalone steaks, pounded
1	egg, well beaten
2	tablespoons milk
	salt and pepper to taste
½	cup flour
	vegetable oil
1	8-ounce can crushed pineapple, drained (optional)
4	ounces champagne (optional)
	paprika

This recipe introduces the famous "double-dip" technique. Place the cheese and ham between the two abalone steaks, and dip the combination in a bowl containing the egg mixed with milk and seasoned with salt and pepper. Then dip the combination into the flour. This is one dip cycle. To double-dip, repeat the cycle, dipping the combination back into the egg, and again into the flour.

Sauté in vegetable oil on both sides until lightly browned—use a double-flip. Then put this double-dipped, double-flipped Cordon Bleu in a preheated 400°F oven for 8 minutes.

This dish may be served with a champagne-pineapple sauce. Combine the pineapple and champagne and place it, in a separate pan, in the oven along with the abalone. The sauce may also be heated in a skillet on the top of the stove if so desired. To serve, pour the heated sauce over the abalone, and garnish with a sprinkle of paprika.

Serves 1. Mitzi thinks this just might be the finest way to prepare abalone.

Ab-burgers

AFTER pounding, grind some abalone steaks in a meat grinder (pounding ground abalone is a pain in the biceps). Add a small amount of chopped onion and a dash of garlic salt. Form into a patty and fry in butter over very low heat until done; that is, when it's just barely beginning to brown, or when you say, "Gee, that looks about done." This can be served as is, or in a bun with whatever you like on a hamburger. If you eat it on a bun, be careful not to add too many condiments or you'll lose the delicate ab flavor. Remember that an ab-burger will not shrink (there is no fat to cook out), and it will tend to be somewhat more filling than ground beef. One whole abalone will make a 'burger that will feed almost anyone. Well, except maybe Pete, but then he's not just anyone. And we can thank the Great Ab in the sky for that.

We once had an ab-burger at a small fish market shack at the end of a pier in Avalon on Santa Catalina Island. A pinch of herbs had been added to the ground abalone. The patty was then very lightly breaded and quickly deep-fried. F-ABulous!

Serve with French fries and Uncola.

Teriyaki Ab

1   teaspoon garlic powder
2   teaspoons red wine vinegar
½   cup sherry
1½ tablespoons sugar
½   cup soy sauce
2   tablespoons chili powder
½   teaspoon dry mustard
1   tablespoon preserved ginger
    abalone steaks, pounded

Mix together all the ingredients except the abalone. Marinate the ab steaks in the mixture for 1 to 2 hours. The marinated steaks may be barbecued on an outdoor grill, turning frequently, until the meat just becomes firm. Depending on the height above the coals, the steaks will be ready in 2 to 3 minutes. The remaining teriyaki mixture may be used for basting. On rainy days bake the steaks in a preheated 400° F oven for 2 minutes, or until heated through. Use a lightweight pan to provide for even cooking.

The seasoning does not smother the ab flavor. Indeed, this recipe seems to strike a balance between a bland, unseasoned abalone and a saucy sweet-and-sour one.

Figure on 6 steaks per person. Another one of our favorites.

Abalone Dirtballs
(Is it really Ab Rumaki?)

> abalone steaks, pounded
> ¼ cup soy sauce
> ¼ cup sake
> 1 8-ounce can water chestnuts
> several strips of bacon
> toothpicks

Mix the soy sauce and sake in a bowl. Slice the steaks into ½-inch-wide strips and soak them in the soy-and sake mixture for 1 to 2 hours. The soy-and-sake mixture has been the subject of some debate. Pete prefers tequila in place of the sake. Purists object to such mixings altogether and use pure soy sauce. Dashwood, an extreme purist, skips the soy sauce and uses pure tequila.

Drain the abalone, wrap a strip around a water chestnut, and stab with a toothpick. This should be done carefully to avoid splitting the chestnut or puncturing the palm of your hand. If the water chestnuts are large, you may want to slice them in half first. Place the abalone dirtballs on a cookie sheet and lay the bacon strips over the abalone. Broil until the bacon starts to crisp. Remove the bacon and feed it to the dog; otherwise it will smother the flavor of the abalone. Remove the dirtballs and serve them to your guests while they are still hot.

Someone once told us the name of this delectable hors d'oeuvre. Unfortunately, it was at a party and Mitzi had a little too much to drink. And if Mitzi had a little too much to drink, the rest of us must have been under some table singing obscene drinking songs.

Pete likes these better than won tons because with the toothpicks they make better weapons at cocktail parties. Red likes 'em because they make better marbles.

Abalone Won Ton

¼ *pound abalone, pounded and ground*
¼ *teaspoon salt*
½ *teaspoon sugar*
½ *teaspoon cornstarch*
2 *tablespoons butter, melted*
1 *small onion, minced*
1 *package won ton skins*

AFTER pounding, grind the abalone and mix all the ingredients except the won ton skins. "Won ton skins?" Yes, they aren't hard to find. Any Japanese food store should have them, and you can find them in most supermarkets, frozen or in the deli case. Place a heaping teaspoonful of the mixture on one won ton skin. Now moisten the sides of the won ton skin and bring all four corners together on the top, to form a bag shape. Squeeze the sides together; they should stick.

Or if you want to do it in the classical Chinese way, fold the filled won ton skin in half to make a triangle. Press edges together. Now take the the two corners by the fold (the base of the triangle) and pull them down and around until they meet and pucker a bit. You know you've done it right if it looks real cute, but if yours looks dumb, you'd better try again.

Repeat the process until all the mixture is used up. Fry the won tons in deep hot oil until the wrappers are brown and crisp, approximately one minute. They make great hot hors d'oeuvre.

Following basic abalone cooking rule no. 3, turn the won tons upside down on paper towels so that any oil that may be inside will drain out.

Fantastic! This combination seems to enhance the abalone's subtle flavor. We've been known to make a whole meal out of them. Serve with Chinese mustard or sweet and sour sauce. Red's favorite.

Ab Chowder

One of your basic problems with ab diving is five divers coming back from a day's diving with a grand slam total of one ab. Everyone sits around staring at each other, thinking "What in the world can we have for dinner with only one ab?" Abalone Chowder should take care of this problem quite tastefully.

4   slices bacon
1   medium onion, diced
1   abalone, pounded
2   cups boiling water
6   small to medium potatoes
3   cups milk
    salt and pepper

First cut the strips of bacon crosswise into small pieces. Drop these into the bottom of a pressure cooker (if you haven't got a pressure cooker, a large pot will do; if you haven't got a large pot, a small pot might do; and if you haven't got a small pot, then God bless you!) and fry until just crisp. Remove the bacon and leave the fat. Fry the onion in the bacon fat. The abalone should be cut into small pieces or ground in a meat grinder—don't forget to observe basic abalone cooking rule no. 1, and pound it FIRST. Drop the abalone into the boiling water for about one minute. Immediately remove the abalone and pour one cup of the water into the pressure cooker. Cut the potatoes into small chunks and add to the contents of the pressure cooker. Cook all under pressure for about 10 minutes. For those of us without pressure cookers, follow the same instructions, but use about 1¾ cups of the water that the abalone was boiled in and boil until the potatoes are done.

Now some of us, including Kurt and Red, have no idea when a potato is done. It's really not that difficult. Just take a fork and stick it into a piece of potato. If it's hard, keep boiling; if the potato falls apart, you're too late; if it goes in easily but firmly, you have reached that fuzzy point called "done."

Let all this cool slightly and add the abalone and milk. Then heat to serving temperature. Under no circumstances boil the soup! If you like thin soup, add a little more milk; for thick soup, use a little less. Salt and pepper to taste. Sprinkle the bits of bacon on top and serve.

With some bread, some cheese, and some wine, this should serve five—and from just one ab!

Easy Soups

A little-known fact is that ocean waves are actually millions of tiny organisms which group together to throw themselves at the diver in an attempt to maim or kill him. Of course, waves can be seen practicing even when divers are not around.

Every now and then we all have one of those days. The waves will cleverly team up with the local rocks to put an eight-inch tear in your wet suit, and you don't want to know what happened inside the suit. After you get back from the hospital, you're in no mood to fix dinner. The following recipes are very good and really easy. The only problem is cleaning and pounding the abalone. With just a little experience, though, this can be done in your sleep. Just ask Kurt, who has been suffering from insomnia lately. He keeps waking up every other day or so. Each of these recipes should feed two people. Add salt and pepper to taste.

1. Cut about ½ pound of pounded abalone into bite-sized chunks. Fry in 3 tablespoons butter over medium heat, and add 1 can (10½ ounces) of cream of chicken soup, 1 soup can of milk, ½ teaspoon paprika, and ⅛ teaspoon nutmeg. Heat and serve.

2. Cut ½ pound of pounded abalone into bite-sized pieces. Just cover with boiling water and cook for 2 minutes, then remove from heat. Pour off enough water to leave 1 cup, and add 1 can of tomato soup and one soup can of milk. Heat and serve.

3. Boil ab as in #2. Add a 13¾-ounce can of chicken broth and ½ cup cream. Heat and serve.

Butter-fried Ab

Now let's suppose 5 divers go out on a boat to about 60 feet of water. From the boat you look down and say, "I'll take that on, and that one, and that one. . . ." Half an hour later you have 20 abs and somebody has to clean them. Take heart— with a little practice this is not too hard. We can clean 20 abs in about 45 minutes, unless Red helps; then it takes about an hour and a half. Pounding takes a little longer, but with a few beers it can seem shorter. The only remaining problem at this point is to consume all that abalone. Butter-fried Ab is the answer.

Slice the steaks into bite-sized pieces and sauté, stirring, in very hot, just short of burning in the pan, margarine for 90 seconds. (We realize it says "butter-fried;" that's a small lie. Actually, it can be done with butter at a lower temperature and much attention to avoid burning. Or you can mix the butter with as much oil. You can then let it get hotter with less danger of burning, although it can still burn under Red's ever attentive chef-like care.)

Each person can eat 1 to 1½ abs. Serve as an entrée with salt, pepper, and Chenin Blanc.

Abalone Sunrise

1   *cup milk*
1   *egg*
1½   *cups whole wheat flour*
½   *teaspoon salt*
       abalone steaks, pounded

Mix together everything except the abalone. Dip each ab steak into some flour and then into the batter. Then cook it just like a regular pancake, or, for more even cooking, fry it in oil.

Surprise someone for breakfast! It looks like a pancake, but tastes like Abalone Sunrise! With butter and syrup, it's great.

You may have noticed the distinct similarity between this recipe and "Red's Steaks." Actually we discovered this one first. While working on an easy steak recipe, Pete tried using a whole wheat flour batter (it was all we had in the house), but it just wasn't quite right. Kurt, who has a basically warped mind, suggested that with syrup it would be great for breakfast. It was! He also suggested that with ketchup it would be good for lunch. It wasn't.

Bar-B-Q Ab

¼   *pound butter*
½   *cup lemon juice*
     pinch pepper and paprika
     abalone steaks, pounded

Melt the butter and add the lemon juice, pepper, and paprika. Stir. Dip each ab steak into this mixture and then place it on the barbecue grill. Turn frequently, basting with the mixture before each turn, cooking until the steak just begins to stiffen.

Six of these per person should be plenty. And for you cowards who really can't handle the out-of-doors, these can also be done in a preheated 400° F oven for 2 minutes in a lightweight pan.

Abalone Creole

1   pound abalone, pounded and cut into
        bite-sized chunks
3   tablespoons butter
½   cup onion, minced
2   tablespoons butter
1   teaspoon celery salt
½   cup green pepper, chopped
1   bay leaf
2   shakes Tabasco sauce*
1   teaspoon salt
1   6-ounce can tomato paste
2½   cups water
1   teaspoon garlic powder
2   tablespoons dry sherry

Fry the abalone over low heat in the 3 tablespoons butter and set aside. Then fry the onion in the 2 tablespoons butter, add the remaining ingredients, and simmer ½ hour. Add the abalone, remove the bay leaf (or some poor clod is sure to eat it), and serve over rice.

Serves 4. Excellent!

*Take caution with the two shakes of Tabasco! A nearly full bottle, and two shakes is almost nothing. A nearly empty bottle and two shakes could be fatal. Try for something in between.

Sweet and Sour Abalone

This may sound somewhat complicated but is in fact quite easy, if you have four arms. But don't worry, the timing is not that important. Just cook over low heat and slowly add everything; it will turn out just great.

6	tablespoons butter
1½	pounds abalone, pounded and cut into bite-sized chunks
2½	cups (a #2 can) pineapple chunks, with liquid
2	tablespoons powdered ginger
1	green pepper, cut into strips
½	cup white wine vinegar
½	cup sugar
	pinch salt
1	tablespoon soy sauce
2½	tablespoons cornstarch

Melt butter and add abalone, cooking over low heat until the pieces begin to firm up. Pour in pineapple with the juice, add ginger, green pepper, vinegar, sugar, salt, and soy sauce. Cook over low heat for 5 minutes.

Spoon out a little of the liquid and mix with the cornstarch until you have a smooth paste. Pour back into the pan and cook it slowly, stirring constantly until the liquid is transparent and slightly thickened.

Served over rice, this should feed 4 people.

Baked Ab

This recipe serves 1, and can be increased for the number of people or quantity of abalone you have.

1	*whole abalone*
	cooking oil
¾	*cup white Chablis*
¼	*cup water*
¼	*teaspoon seasoned salt*
¼	*teaspoon paprika*
½	*tablespoon lemon juice*

Take the ab after cleaning but before slicing, and lightly pound the whole thing. The pounding should be just enough to make the ab limp, yet not enough to split it. This is the secret. Preheat the oven to 300° F. Lightly brown both sides of the abalone in cooking oil, and then place it in a casserole (Red says that's just a covered ovenproof pot) with all the other ingredients. Bake, covered, in the 300° oven for about 1½ hours. Serve the ab on a platter surrounded by a garnish.

And Red said it would never be possible to bake an ab and have it come out tasting good. But this recipe works. If you can find a very small apple, stuff it in the ab's mouth. If sliced very thin, under appropriate party conditions this dish could serve 387.

perlemoen

("Abalone under Gas")

This is a prized recipe of Jennifer Voerhoef of Cape Town, South Africa, where abs are called "perlemoen." We tested it, and think it's great. If you're REALLY lazy, this is the recipe for you, because you don't have to pound the abalone! The pressure cooker is the secret.

4	*tablespoons butter*
1½	*pounds UNPOUNDED abalone, cut into thin slices*
2½	*cups white wine*
4	*ounces heavy cream*
1	*teaspoon ground nutmeg*
	salt and pepper to taste
1	*tablespoon cornstarch mixed with a small amount of water or wine*

In a pressure cooker, melt the butter and add unpounded abalone. We realize that this violates basic abalone cooking rule no. 1, but the pressure cooker tenderizes it for you. Cook this for 5 minutes under pressure. Remove from heat, decompress, add the wine, and cook again for 15-20 minutes under pressure. Remove from heat.

Add the cream, nutmeg, salt, pepper, and cornstarch, and cook over low heat, stirring constantly until thick. Be sure not to boil it once you've added the cream, or it will curdle.

Serves 3-4.

Abalone Marsala

("Haliotis in Cheap Wine")

In this recipe, the onions and mushrooms are optional—some cooks use more wine in place of them. In fact, some use more wine in place of the water, the bouillon, the flour, the salt and pepper.

8-10	abalone steaks, pounded
½	cup flour
2	tablespoons butter
2	tablespoons cooking oil
½	medium onion, chopped or sliced and separated into rings (optional)
10-12	mushrooms, sliced (optional)
	salt and pepper to taste
¾	cup water
1	beef or chicken bouillon cube
¼	cup marsala, madeira, sherry, or any other favorite fortified wine

Lightly but thoroughly coat the abalone with flour. In a saucepan, melt 1 tablespoon of the butter in the cooking oil over medium heat. When the foam has subsided, brown the abalone for less than a minute on each side.

Remove the abalone to a warm plate. Reduce the heat to low and add the remaining butter to the pan along with the onion, mushrooms, salt, and pepper, and simmer for about 5 minutes to soften the onion. Then add the water and bouillon cube to the pan and stir until the cube is dissolved.

Now the object will not be to drown the abalone, but to slowly smother it, so the sauce needs to be thickened. Put about ¼ cup of the sauce into a small bowl, and make a smooth paste with about ¼-⅓ of the flour you have left from coating the abalone. You can then blend it back into the sauce in the pan without forming any lumps, clumps, or glumps of flour—smooooooth.

Finally, add the wine and all the abalone steaks. Simmer for 3 minutes or so, and serve.

Serves 2.

Abalone Thermidor

1	pound abalone, pounded and diced
1	cup boiling water
½	cup cream
½	teaspoon paprika
	pinch celery salt
1	shake Tabasco sauce*
2	tablespoons cornstarch
3	tablespoons butter
1½	cups white bread, shredded
	salt and pepper to taste

Place the diced abalone in the boiling water, and remove from heat after one minute. Let cool slightly and add the cream, paprika, celery salt, and Tabasco. Simmer 5 minutes. Spoon out some of the liquid and add to the cornstarch, stirring to make a smooth paste. Combine this with the other mixture, and simmer another 5 minutes, stirring. Preheat your broiler. Melt the butter and add to the shredded white bread, stirring until all the butter is absorbed.

Place the abalone mixture in a shallow pan, and put the bread on top. Place in the broiler until the bread is browned. Salt and pepper to taste.

Serves three.

Please believe us, this is Abalone Thermidor, not Lobster Thermidor. This is better.

*One shake out of a full Tabasco bottle gives no flavor. One shake out of an almost empty bottle makes it hot. No, very hot.

Abalone Newberg

1   *pound abalone, pounded and diced*
6   *tablespoons butter*
¼   *cup dry sherry*
½   *teaspoon paprika*
½   *teaspoon nutmeg*
3   *egg yolks*
1   *cup cream*
    salt and pepper to taste

Sauté the abalone in the butter over low heat. Add the sherry and simmer for 2 minutes. In a bowl, combine all other ingredients and beat. Add to the abalone and cook until the mixture is thick, but do not boil. Salt and pepper to taste.

Poured over toast, this should serve three.

Now, don't expect this to taste like Lobster Newberg. If it did, we'd call it Lobster Newberg.

71

·❦A ℬ-DENDUM❦.

If you ask the Japanese how to cook abalone, they'll say, "Sashimi, not steak." At the beach they just pry the ab out of its shell, trim it, slice it, and "dip it in soy sauce and drink sake."

Some people "cook" abalone by simply marinating un-pounded strips in lemon or lime juice. We have had very good "pickled ab," but when we try such a recipe, we end up with chewy lemon or lime juice.

If we ever open that restaurant, Red wants to make a Stuffed Abalone Meunière, filled with shrimp and crab and smothered in a white sauce. The problem is that Red wants to do this with an Ab-O-Matic Quicko Meunière Maker.

We really wanted to call this the "Complete Abalone Cookbook," but the delicate flavor is so versatile that it would be impossible to exhaust its culinary combinations. Just think of the various chicken and veal recipes which might be adapted for abalone, if you are careful to avoid those that overpower the ab's subtle flavor. And unfortunately for you true gourmets, we were unable to come up with a really good recipe for abalone tongues.

" They taste pretty good, but I think
we forgot to peel 'em "

Abalone is indeed a most versatile meat. Its delicate flavor is in such great demand that its population off the California coast is dwindling. Abalone processing plants once dotted the entire coastline. Now only three or four operators work sporadically according to a fluctuating supply.

Of course, we can always blame pollution. Especially along the mainland, resulting poor water quality has obliterated some kelp forests with all their dependent fauna. But to turn ecology over to the radical ecologists is like turning religion over to the Inquisition. What can a lone diver do? Pick up a beer can. Throw it at a pollutocrat!

Of course, we can always blame the sea otters. Now reestablishing themselves along the coast of California, these fun-loving critters spend more time eating than we do sleeping. In spite of any claims by otter conservation organizations, sea otters can devastate an abalone population if given enough little rocks. They cleverly use these rocks to pound a hole in an ab's shell and pull out its meat. The Department of Fish and Game does not advocate "harvesting" otters to help control the potential destruction of many marine fisheries. They contend that the commercial abalone fishery was founded on "overabundance" which resulted from the population explosion of abalone after the otter's near extinction. This analysis must be incomplete, since the California Indians once enjoyed

74

hunting both abalone and otters, then plentiful. And cabezons, crabs, and octopuses also eat abalone.

Of course, we can always blame it on Pete. There is little doubt that a major cause of the decline in the abalone population along the Southern California coast is due to overfishing by both sport divers and commercial fishermen. Localized closures of selected areas for at least 5 years, or a state-wide moratorium on ab fishing for perhaps as long as a decade may be required to repopulate the abalone's coastal habitat. A reseeding program is only now gaining momentum, but should have been implemented long ago. We are now overfishing, bagging more than a "maximum sustained yield."

New mariculture techniques are now being applied which may soon enable us to harvest large crops of homegrown abalones. Such laboratory farms can protect the young abs from their natural predators in the sea. Farming is conceivable, since the abalone is a very hardy animal, much more resistant to disease than other marine fauna. Of course, with all the good stuff in its blood, you would expect this. Abalone even grow well when planted on the legs of offshore oil rigs. Dr. Dave has a SCARF program (no, we did not suggest the name; it stands for Southern California Abalone Research Facility), which is the aquacultural center of the Ocean Studies Institute which he directs. If marine aquaculture is going to help supply the world's protein, abalone farming is a natural first step. In the food chain, an abalone is at a more efficient level than a cow. Abalone can be reared in reasonable-sized tanks, and they don't swim too far from where they're "planted." Ab meat is now priced high enough to encourage the investment of the funds needed to establish the program. The problem is time. It takes longer to grow an abalone than it does to raise a cow. Seven years' work can be eaten at one meal.

What can we do now? Be respectful of the few limitations we have imposed upon ourselves as a community. And be disrespectful of those divers who ignore them. Support stiffer penalties for the illegal taking of abalone. ABstain. Eat more one-ab chowder. Talk to a sea otter and try to convince him not to take shorts. Naturally, we have never taken a short. Well, there was that daughter of the Fish & Game warden. . .

APPENDIX

After your gourmet meal you probably discovered that you now have a large number of shells. We usually throw them into the back yard and let the dog play with them. But sometimes we want to save the better ones to clean up for ornaments and gifts, ashtrays and spittoons.

Unfortunately, when the shells come out of the sea they look and smell disgusting. An untold number of li'l critters living on these shells die when out of the water, and stink. So don't leave your shells lying around the kitchen overnight if you ever want to go into the kitchen again. With a mere 2 or 3 hours of work these shells are readily polished up. 2 or 3 hours!?! Well, there is an easier way. The shells don't come out as well, but we always try the easy way first.

In this method, use any pointed tool, like an ice pick, to break the barnacles and other assorted growths off the back of the shell. Next, coat the inside of the shell with paraffin. Now dump the shell into diluted muriatic acid, which you can get at any swimming pool supply store. Eye protection is a must, and you should wear old clothes, unless you like acid burns in your tuxedo. Remove the shell from the acid with rubber gloves, and rinse it thoroughly in cold water. To remove the paraffin, place the shell on its back in a pan of water. Put the pan on the stove and heat until simmering. Remove from heat and let cool. Skim the solidified paraffin off the top and remove the shell from the water. Coating the shell with mineral oil is probably the best method for preserving the shine.

For you pros, there is a harder way. This produces better-looking shells, but it does take several hours and much elbow grease. Take an ice pick again, and a wire brush, and scrape, brush, and chisel the back of the shell until it is cleaned off. We suggest that you don't grind or sand the shells. The very fine dust might be toxic and could cause pulmonary problems. Occasionally brush muriatic acid on the back, let it set for a few minutes and then rinse it off. After you have removed all of the assorted junk from the shell, coat the outside with surfacing resin and the inside with mineral oil. Or you can brush it with varathane.

Finally, there is Red's method, unquestionably the easiest. He gave his shells to his boss, Brad, with some Tom Sawyer-like story about the aphrodisiac qualities of polishing ab shells. After all, abalone do it on one foot.

BIBLIOGRAPHY

Ashkenazy, Irvin. "The Abalone." *Oceans* 5 (1972): 56-61.

Barada, Bill. "Abalone an Endangered Species." *Skin Diver Magazine* 23, no. 6 (1974): 53-57.

Brown, Joseph E. "New Hope for the Sirloin of the Sea." *Oceans* 4 (1971): 56-63.

Cox, Keith W. *California Abalones, Family Haliotidae.* State of California: The Resources Agency, Department of Fish and Game; Fish Bulletin 118 (1962). (Source of the map on page 13 and chart on page 26.)

Fleming, Ian. *You Only Live Twice.* New York: New American Library, 1964.

Frey, Herbert W., ed. "Abalone." *California's Living Marine Resources and Their Utilization.* State of California: The Resources Agency, Department of Fish and Game (1971): 31-33.

Gibson, Mark E. "Abalones of the World." *Skin Diver Magazine* 24, no. 5 (1975): 40-42.

Howorth, Peter. "American Abalone." *Oceans* 5 (1972): 62-65.

Leighton, David L. "Observations of the effect of diet on shell coloration in red abalone, *Haliotis rufescens* Swainson." *The Veliger*, Vol. 4, no. 1 (1961): 29-32.

Miyamoto, T. *Ama: The Women Sea Divers in Japan* (1962).

Owen, Buzz; Mclean, James H.; and Meyer, Richard J. *Hybridization in the Eastern Pacific Abalones (Haliotis)*. Los Angeles: Bulletin of the Los Angeles County Museum of Natural History, Publications in Science, no. 9 (1971).

Scholl, D.W., and Smith, L.O. "Manna from the Sea." *Skin Diver Magazine* 5, no. 7 (1956): 26-29.